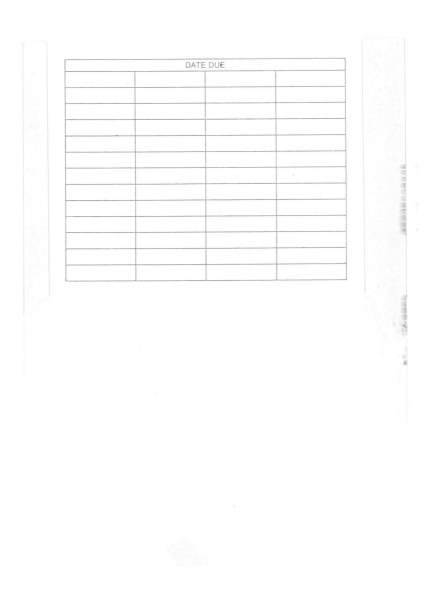

| DATE DUE | | | |
|---|---|---|---|
| | | | |
| | | | |
| | | | |
| | | | |
| | | | |
| | | | |
| | | | |
| | | | |
| | | | |
| | | | |
| | | | |
| | | | |
| | | | |
| | | | |

# SPORTS GREAT CHARLES BARKLEY

*Revised Edition*

# —Sports Great Books—

## BASEBALL

**Sports Great Jim Abbott**
*0-89490-395-0/ Savage*

**Sports Great Barry Bonds**
*0-89490-595-3/ Sullivan*

**Sports Great Bobby Bonilla**
*0-89490-417-5/ Knapp*

**Sports Great Orel Hershiser**
*0-89490-389-6/ Knapp*

**Sports Great Bo Jackson**
*0-89490-281-4/ Knapp*

**Sports Great Greg Maddux**
*0-89490-873-1/ Thornley*

**Sports Great Kirby Puckett**
*0-89490-392-6/ Aaseng*

**Sports Great Cal Ripken, Jr.**
*0-89490-387-X/ Macnow*

**Sports Great Nolan Ryan**
*0-89490-394-2/ Lace*

**Sports Great Darryl Strawberry**
*0-89490-291-1/ Torres & Sullivan*

## BASKETBALL

**Sports Great Charles Barkley**
**Revised Edition**
*0-7660-1004-X/ Macnow*

**Sports Great Larry Bird**
*0-89490-368-3/ Kavanagh*

**Sports Great Muggsy Bogues**
*0-89490-876-6/ Rekela*

**Sports Great Patrick Ewing**
*0-89490-369-1/ Kavanagh*

**Sports Great Anfernee Hardaway**
*0-89490-758-1/ Rekela*

**Sports Great Magic Johnson**
**Revised and Expanded**
*0-89490-348-9/ Haskins*

**Sports Great Michael Jordan**
**Revised Edition**
*0-89490-978-9/ Aaseng*

**Sports Great Jason Kidd**
*0-7660-1001-5/ Torres*

**Sports Great Karl Malone**
*0-89490-599-6/ Savage*

**Sports Great Reggie Miller**
*0-89490-874-X/ Thornley*

**Sports Great Alonzo Mourning**
*0-89490-875-8/ Fortunato*

**Sports Great Hakeem Olajuwon**
*0-89490-372-1/ Knapp*

**Sports Great Shaquille O'Neal**
**Revised Edition**
*0-7660-1003-1/ Sullivan*

**Sports Great Scottie Pippen**
*0-89490-755-7/ Bjarkman*

**Sports Great David Robinson**
**Revised Edition**
*0-7660-1077-5/ Aaseng*

**Sports Great Dennis Rodman**
*0-89490-759-X/ Thornley*

**Sports Great John Stockton**
*0-89490-598-8/ Aaseng*

**Sports Great Isiah Thomas**
*0-89490-374-8/ Knapp*

**Sports Great Dominique Wilkins**
*0-89490-754-9/ Bjarkman*

## FOOTBALL

**Sports Great Troy Aikman**
*0-89490-593-7/ Macnow*

**Sports Great Jerome Bettis**
*0-89490-872-3/Majewski*

**Sports Great John Elway**
*0-89490-282-2/ Fox*

**Sports Great Brett Favre**
*0-7660-1000-7/ Savage*

**Sports Great Jim Kelly**
*0-89490-670-4/ Harrington*

**Sports Great Joe Montana**
*0-89490-371-3/ Kavanagh*

**Sports Great Jerry Rice**
*0-89490-419-1/ Dickey*

**Sports Great Barry Sanders**
*0-89490-418-3/ Knapp*

**Sports Great Emmitt Smith**
*0-7660-1002-3/ Grabowski*

**Sports Great Herschel Walker**
*0-89490-207-5/ Benagh*

## HOCKEY

**Sports Great Wayne Gretzky**
*0-89490-757-3/ Rappoport*

**Sports Great Mario Lemieux**
*0-89490-596-1/ Knapp*

**Sports Great Eric Lindros**
*0-89490-871-5/ Rappoport*

## TENNIS

**Sports Great Steffi Graf**
*0-89490-597-X/ Knapp*

**Sports Great Pete Sampras**
*0-89490-756-5/ Sherrow*

# SPORTS GREAT CHARLES BARKLEY

*Revised Edition*

## Glen Macnow

*—Sports Great Books—*

**Enslow Publishers, Inc.**

40 Industrial Road        PO Box 38
Box 398                Aldershot
Berkeley Heights, NJ 07922   Hants GU12 6BP
USA                        UK

http://www.enslow.com

**Library of Congress Cataloging-in-Publication Data**

Macnow, Glen.
    Sports great Charles Barkley / Glen Macnow. — Rev. ed.
      p. cm. — (Sports great books)
    Includes index.
    Summary: Profiles the personal life and professional career of the basketball player
nicknamed "The Round Mound of Rebound" early in his career but considered today
to be one of the best power forwards in NBA history.
    ISBN 0-7660-1004-X
    1. Barkley, Charles, 1963– —Juvenile literature. 2. Basketball players—United
States—Biography—Juvenile literature. [1. Barkley, Charles, 1963– . 2. Basketball
players. 3. Afro-Americans—Biography.] I. Title. II. Series.
GV 884.B28M33 1998
796.323'092
[B]—DC21                              97-22844
                                              CIP
                                              AC

Printed in the United States of America

10 9 8 7 6 5 4 3 2

**To Our Readers:**
All Internet addresses in this book were active and appropriate when we went to press. Any
comments or suggestions can be sent by e-mail to Comments@enslow.com or to the address
on the back cover.

**Illustration Credits:** Auburn University, p. 20; Bill Baptist, p. 59; Mike
Maicher/Philadelphia 76ers, pp. 17, 22, 25, 31, 35; NBA Photos/Andrew D.
Bernstein, pp. 45, 48; NBA Photos/Andy Hayt, pp. 10, 12, 38; NBA Photos/Barry
Gossage, p. 50; NBA Photos/Chris Corvatta, pp. 41, 53, 56; NBA Photos/Scott
Cunningham, p. 8; Zack Hill, p. 27.

**Cover Illustration:** NBA Photos/Scott Cunningham

# Contents

*Chapter 1* . . . . . . . . . . . . . . . . . . . . . . . . . . . . 7

*Chapter 2* . . . . . . . . . . . . . . . . . . . . . . . . . . 15

*Chapter 3* . . . . . . . . . . . . . . . . . . . . . . . . . . 24

*Chapter 4* . . . . . . . . . . . . . . . . . . . . . . . . . . 33

*Chapter 5* . . . . . . . . . . . . . . . . . . . . . . . . . . 43

*Chapter 6* . . . . . . . . . . . . . . . . . . . . . . . . . . 52

*Career Statistics* . . . . . . . . . . . . . . . . . . . . . . . 61

*Where to Write* . . . . . . . . . . . . . . . . . . . . . . . 62

*Index* . . . . . . . . . . . . . . . . . . . . . . . . . . . . . 63

# Chapter 1

Game 3 of the 1993 National Basketball Association (NBA) Finals was in double overtime when Phoenix Suns coach Paul Westphal called a time-out. Just eight seconds remained on the clock. The Suns were down by two points to the Chicago Bulls. They had to score—now—or they would lose the game.

Westphal gathered his players around him for a quick strategy session. Would he run a complicated play designed to fool the Bulls? Would he tell his players to pass the ball around until one of them had an open shot? Or would he have them kick the ball out to Dan Majerle, the team's top three-point shooter, for a chance to win the game? No, Westphal's plan was simpler than all that. "Give the ball to Charles," the coach told his players. "And then everyone else get out of the way. He is our go-to guy."

So point guard Kevin Johnson passed the ball in to Charles Barkley, basketball's one-man wrecking crew. As the other Suns backed away, Barkley drove toward the net. He dribbled past Michael Jordan, the NBA's top superstar.

When Charles Barkley decides to take the ball to the basket, it is almost impossible to stop him.

Barkley then leaped into the air and was challenged by Horace Grant, one of basketball's best defensive players. Barkley just pushed Grant away as if he were swatting a mosquito and slammed the ball through the hoop. Later, Grant said that he felt as if he had been run over by a truck.

Barkley's slam dunk tied the game as the buzzer sounded the end of the second overtime. Inspired by his move, the Suns controlled the third overtime period and won the game, 129–121, at Chicago Stadium. Barkley finished with 24 points and 19 rebounds. Not bad for someone whose aching elbow had been drained of fluid thirty minutes before the opening tip-off.

"Charles was the difference tonight," said teammate Danny Ainge. "And I'm not just talking about his scoring. His leadership kept us alive." For example, Ainge said, Barkley gathered around his teammates during each break throughout the overtimes. He patted them on the back and praised their efforts. He even cracked a few jokes to keep everyone loose.

A great player, a clutch performer, and an inspiring teammate—each describes Charles Barkley during his NBA career, and especially, during the 1992–93 season. That was his first season with the Suns after spending eight seasons with the Philadelphia 76ers. He was voted the league's Most Valuable Player (MVP) that year after leading the Suns to a league-best record of 62 wins and 20 losses. He averaged more than 25 points and 12 rebounds per game. More importantly, perhaps, he brought a fighting spirit to a team that had boasted of good talent for years, but seemed to lack leadership.

The Suns cruised past the Los Angeles Lakers, the San Antonio Spurs, and the Seattle SuperSonics on their way to meeting the Bulls in the 1993 Finals. Barkley injured his elbow diving for a loose ball early in the postseason. It hurt so

Charles Barkley shoots over the outstretched arms of San Antonio Spurs' center David Robinson. The Spurs were one of the teams the Suns defeated on their way to the 1993 NBA Finals.

much that it kept him up nights for a month. Still, he never stopped hustling and he never sat out.

"I want a championship so much," he said. "They could cut my arm off and I'm still not going to miss this." Alas, it did not happen. The Suns lost the first two championship series games, at home, before winning the thrilling triple-overtime game at Chicago Stadium. In Game 4, Barkley scored 42 points and pulled down 13 rebounds. However, Jordan also scored 42 points for Chicago, and the Bulls won the game. The Suns rallied to win Game 5, but the Bulls came back to win the series in six games.

The Bulls had won the NBA title the two previous years, so no one was surprised by their "Three-peat." Yet the Suns showed that they were a team of heart and character. And Barkley—cracking jokes when he wasn't cracking opponents' bones—reminded everyone that a great player can have fun on the court.

Michael Jordan was named the Most Valuable Player for the 1993 Finals. Accepting his award, he said, "I'm just glad that we don't have to play Barkley anymore. He doesn't just beat you, he beats you up."

Barkley spent four seasons in Phoenix before being traded to the Houston Rockets prior to the start of the 1996–97 season. By then, he was thirty-three years old and slowing down a little bit. "He may not be quite the superstar talent he was a few years ago," Houston coach Rudy Tomjanovich said the day of the trade. "But I don't think he's lost one ounce of his desire."

Desire? No one would ever doubt Charles Barkley's desire. He is neither the tallest player in the NBA nor the fastest—but he is one of the best. He does not possess Shawn Kemp's classic shooting touch, nor Penny Hardaway's lightning-quick

After four seasons with the Phoenix Suns, Charles Barkley was traded to the Houston Rockets in 1996.

moves, nor Michael Jordan's ability to fly. Still, he is a star among stars. The main reason is his thirst for success.

"Charles hates losing so much that I've seen his eyes turn red after a bad game," said Tom Chambers, a teammate in Phoenix. "He's the only guy I've ever seen who can scare his teammates into playing better."

From an early age, Charles Wade Barkley was determined to do his best. He practiced harder than the players around him and carefully studied the game when he wasn't playing. When he ran up against an obstacle, he did not give up. Instead, he tried twice as hard and worked until he was able to accomplish the goal.

For instance, when Charles was fifteen, he was told that he was too short and too fat to play on the high school basketball team. The coach said that Charles could not jump high enough to be a good player.

When Charles heard that, he decided that maybe he couldn't teach himself to grow, but he could teach himself to jump. He spent hours every day hopping over a fence in his backyard in Leeds, Alabama. The jumping helped him lose weight and become more athletic. Soon he made the team. After a while, he became a starter. Finally, he won a scholarship to Auburn University.

Years later, Barkley was again told that he was too short. His style of play in college was to crash the boards, to stand near the basket and dare opponents to push away his 300-pound body. He is built a lot like a refrigerator—and it's very difficult to move a refrigerator.

Upon entering the NBA in 1984, many experts thought that Barkley was not tall enough to play under the basket. He stands just under six feet six inches tall. Meanwhile, the average player in the NBA is six-feet nine-inches, and almost every team has a player who stands taller than seven feet.

These giants usually control the play of the game, stuffing the basketball and grabbing the rebounds.

Barkley, the experts said, would have to change his style of play. It was believed that a man his size could never be a good inside player in the pros. The experts were wrong. During the 1986–87 season, Barkley became the shortest player in the forty-year history of the NBA to lead the league in rebounds. Six years later, he was the league's MVP. Five times, he was voted a first-stringer on the All-NBA team. Some day he will be a member of the Basketball Hall of Fame.

Standing still, the chunky Barkley does not look like the kind of player who can be a force in basketball. Yet when Barkley starts to move, he can do remarkable things: and when he speaks, you begin to understand that his heart is what makes him so great. He just wants to succeed more than the other players. His exciting style of play has been described as being like a bottle of soda pop that someone shakes until it explodes all over the court.

"My momma told me long ago to let my emotions out," Barkley once said. "And she told me to always try my best. I've lived by those rules my whole life. If you don't try your best, what's the point of trying at all?"

# Chapter 2

In the broiling summertime heat of Leeds, Alabama, a fifteen-year-old boy spent hours every day challenging a chain-link fence. The determined teenager would run at the four-foot-high fence and try to leap over it. Sometimes, he didn't make it, skinning his knees or banging his elbows. His mother said he looked like someone who had gotten in a car crash. Still, he practiced and practiced for months. Finally, he was able to stand next to the fence and hop over it flat-footed.

The boy was Charles Wade Barkley, then known as Wade to his friends. At that time, the summer before his junior year of high school, he stood five feet ten inches tall. The high school basketball coach, Billy Coupland, had told Wade that if he didn't grow, his chances of making the team were not good. Wade desperately wanted to make the team. So he decided he would just have to learn to outjump the taller boys.

He spent hours every day hopping back and forth over that backyard fence. He taught himself to jump, and at the same time he did begin to grow. By the winter, he had sprouted to six-feet two-inches and won a starting position on the Leeds High School team.

Charles was born in Leeds on February 20, 1963. His parents were divorced when he was a baby. His father moved away to California and stopped seeing Charles. A few years later, Charles's mom Charcey married a man named Clee Glenn and had two other sons. When Charles was eleven, Mr. Glenn was killed in a car crash. So Charles lost two fathers as a child, which is tough for any kid to handle.

Charles's grandparents, Adolphus and Johnnie Edwards, helped raise him. And today, Charles's most special relationship is with his grandmother. She gives him advice on everything from raising his own daughter to dealing with NBA referees to handling the responsibilities of being a celebrity.

Barkley's mother recalls that her son was so determined to become a star that, as a teenager, he didn't have time for anything else but running, practicing, and playing basketball. "He would run for hours in the hot sun," Mrs. Glenn said. "And he'd jump and jump over that fence. I'd watch him fall down and hurt himself, and I would want him to stop. But he told me, 'Momma, I'm going to play in the NBA.' And he meant it. Nothing was going to stop him."

Charles and his mother believed in his dream—even if no one else did. Most of the time, Charles was only an average high school player. His leaping skills made him great at blocking shots and grabbing rebounds. His own shots, however, were often off target, and he had trouble dribbling and passing the ball to teammates. In his junior year, Charles was just the third- or fourth-best player on the Leeds High team, said the coach. He averaged 13 points and 11 rebounds a game. Leeds won 25 games while losing just 7.

Barkley grew to six feet four inches as a high school

Though he is shorter than most other NBA power forwards, Barkley is still able to perform rim-rattling dunks. This is because of his amazing jumping ability. As a boy, Barkley practiced jumping every day to make up for his lack of height.

senior. And his hours of practice began to pay off. He started grabbing offensive rebounds and jamming them through the hoop in one motion. One night, he pulled down 30 rebounds in a game against rival Ensley High. Overall, he averaged 19 points and 18 rebounds a game. Leeds went 26–3 and was invited to play in a Christmas tournament in Tuscaloosa, Alabama. Dozens of coaches and scouts came to the tournament to watch Bobby Lee Hurt, a tall center who was regarded as the best high school player in the state. Yet when Hurt came up against Barkley, the state suddenly had a new best player.

Barkley had 25 points and 20 rebounds in a game against Hurt, leading Leeds High to victory. He blocked several of Hurt's shots and held the taller player to 20 points and just 9 rebounds. Now the scouts were excited about this new player, the chubby forward from Leeds who could jump to the sky.

Colleges from around the South started to offer scholarships. Barkley chose Auburn University because it was near his home. He wasn't ready to leave his family, telling friends that he was "still a baby." What he meant was that he was seventeen years old, but he was not prepared for living away from the people he loved.

That was OK with Barkley's mom. Charcey Glenn worked hard cleaning houses when Barkley was growing up. Her son helped by taking care of their house—washing, cooking, and ironing the clothes. He even changed all the bedsheets twice a week. He wanted to make life easier for his mother and often promised her that he would one day become rich playing basketball and buy her everything she wanted. She never tried to talk him out of his goal.

First, though, Barkley had to deal with the pressures of college. At Auburn University, the basketball coach was Sonny Smith. He was the toughest coach for whom Barkley ever played. Smith demanded hard work and top results from his players. Anyone who failed to follow Smith's rules faced strong punishment—as Barkley would soon find out.

From the start, Barkley and Smith did not get along. Barkley had grown to just under six feet five inches, but his weight had grown even more. He had entered college at 260 pounds, but he liked the food so much that his weight quickly grew to 300 pounds. Fans and opponents found Barkley's shape something to laugh at. They gave him nicknames like "Boy Gorge," "The Round Mound of Rebound," and "Bread Truck." In some arenas, fans threw empty pizza boxes from the seats to make fun of his eating habits. One time, as a joke, someone had a meal delivered to Barkley on the Auburn bench.

Coach Smith found none of these things funny. He felt that Barkley's weight slowed him down and caused him to lose energy. The coach tried to make Barkley work harder at practice, but Barkley wanted to push himself only in games that really counted. Smith told Barkley to lay off the snacks and go to class. Barkley did neither.

During practice one day, Smith screamed at Barkley to "do something." So the next time down the court, Barkley jammed in a rebound so hard that it snapped the rim from the backboard. On another occasion, Smith had Barkley run "gut-churner" drills with the Auburn football team. Players had to run up and down stadium steps until they quit or threw up. Barkley did neither, but he kept running.

In another try to make Barkley lose weight, Smith had him run with heavy cinder blocks on his back. He made Barkley run laps around the gym and roll fifty yards, back and forth, on the football field. Once, Smith made Barkley run a mile with a bucket of water in each hand.

The plan didn't work. Barkley kept gaining weight. Yet he

Barkley during his days at Auburn University.

also kept improving as a player. In one memorable game against the tough Georgetown Hoyas, Barkley did the impossible. He blocked a shot by Georgetown center Patrick Ewing, who stood six inches taller than Barkley. In that contest, Barkley scored 24 points and snared 16 rebounds. His performance wasn't enough, however, as Georgetown won.

In three seasons at Auburn, Barkley averaged 14.1 points and 9.6 rebounds a game. As a junior in 1984, he was the Southeastern Conference Player of the Year and helped the Tigers to their first NCAA tournament berth. The "Round Mound," extra weight and all, became a national sensation. Here was a chunky kid who set shot-blocking and rebounding records and developed such a soft shooting touch that he made 64 percent of his shots over his college career.

A few years later, Coach Smith admitted that he had been too hard on Barkley. Smith said that Barkley was not used to discipline and did not like it. Still, the coach felt that some of his toughness had helped Barkley. It taught Barkley how to push himself to be as great as he wanted to be.

Toward the end of his junior year, Barkley went on a diet. He slimmed down to a muscular dynamo of 265 pounds who could thunder through opponents. And he began to think about another important decision. After his great college season, Barkley knew he could leave Auburn and become a first-round pick in the pro basketball draft. His family needed the money he would earn, and it would be a chance to realize a lifelong dream. Besides, his relationship with Coach Smith did not seem likely to improve.

He also wanted to remain in college and work toward earning his degree. Everyone at Auburn, and basketball fans from around Alabama, were hoping he would stay. They felt the school could become a national champion if Barkley was there to lead the team.

After his junior year at Auburn University, Barkley was named the Southeastern Conference Player of the Year. Soon after, the Philadelphia 76ers took him with the fifth selection in the 1984 NBA draft.

Barkley was torn. In the end, he decided that the chance to go pro and be drafted early was too good to pass up. So he applied for the NBA June draft. As the day neared, Barkley wondered which team would select him.

The 1984 NBA draft will always be remembered as one of the best in the league's history. Hakeem Olajuwon, the giant center from Nigeria, was picked first by the Houston Rockets. Michael Jordan soon followed, going to the Chicago Bulls. Other fine players coming out of that draft included Sam Perkins, Alvin Robertson, and John Stockton. The Philadelphia 76ers had the fifth pick in that year's draft. Their choice: Auburn forward Charles Barkley.

# *Chapter 3*

Barkley was thrilled to go to Philadelphia. Back then, the 76ers, the Boston Celtics, and the Los Angeles Lakers were regarded as the best teams in the league.

Before that afternoon in June, Barkley had expected to go to a weak team. In the NBA, the teams that lose the most games get the first draft picks after the season. That means that most great college players get chosen by bad teams. They must learn to play pro ball in a losing atmosphere. The 76ers made a trade to get the first-round pick of the Los Angeles Clippers. That turned out to be the fifth pick overall—and they grabbed Barkley.

The 76ers were a team of stars during Barkley's rookie season. Julius Erving, better known as "Dr. J," started at one forward spot. Erving's high-flying style and slam dunks made him the most exciting player in basketball. The center was Moses Malone, a mountain-sized man who led the NBA in rebounding six different seasons. Sharpshooter Andrew Toney started at one guard spot, and reliable Maurice Cheeks started at the other. The other forward was Bobby

As a rookie, Barkley (34) got the chance to play with Moses Malone (2), one of the greatest centers in basketball history.

Jones, a defensive wizard who was nearing the end of a solid twelve-year career.

Into this mix came Barkley. The 76ers' thinking was simple: They wanted a good rebounder who could help Malone under the basket. And they wanted an exciting player who could come off the bench to replace Jones midway through the game and score some points. Barkley seemed perfect for both jobs.

When the 1984–85 season began, Barkley quickly learned that he was as talented as the NBA's top veterans. That part of the job wasn't as hard as he expected. Instead, the toughest part of being a pro was getting used to life away from his family. Life on the road in the NBA is different from life with a college team. The season is much longer and pro players have no coaches or teachers to "baby-sit" for them. They must make their own decisions and take care of themselves. Barkley rented an apartment in downtown Philadelphia. Still, he called his mother almost every day to ask her advice.

Among teammates, his closest friend was Julius Erving, who had already played thirteen years as a pro. Dr. J saw Barkley as a player in his own mold. Comparing the way Barkley played as a first-year player to the way he played, Erving said, "He just needs to be given some sneakers and pointed in the right direction."

So Erving took the young rookie aside at least once a week for private lessons. The teaching included topics such as how to use the head fake and when to take a foul. And it went beyond that. Erving taught Barkley how to lead life as a pro. He taught the rookie how to stay in shape and stay out of trouble. And he explained what duties go along with great talent. A star player, Erving said, must always know how to behave himself on—and off—the court.

Barkley became a fan favorite within weeks of joining the

Barkley's exciting style of play and flamboyant personality made him a fan favorite in Philadelphia.

76ers. The club, although talented, was getting older and playing without much zip. Barkley played with the joy of a little boy. He never stopped running, diving after loose balls, and shouting at players on other teams. Sometimes, he acted more like a football player than a basketball player. The 76ers' fans cheered his every move. "When Charles is in there, our whole team picks up," said Billy Cunningham, who was Philadelphia's coach. "He's like adding a lit match to a few sticks of dynamite."

Still, Barkley made some rookie mistakes. He daydreamed during games. And he played lazy defense at times. He had never been a great defensive player. Even today, he admits that guarding the other team's players is his least-favorite part of the game. Barkley insists that he can play tough defense when he has to. He just doesn't like to.

In one game against the Detroit Pistons during his first season, Barkley forgot to cover the Pistons' center Bill Laimbeer. That allowed Laimbeer to score a few easy baskets. "Help, Charles, help!" Coach Cunningham shouted. "Get your mind in the game!" Barkley bowed his head like a student caught napping in class, but he quickly woke up. He grabbed the next rebound, dribbled past three opponents, and slam-dunked the basketball. The Philadelphia fans went nuts.

In the 1985 playoffs, Barkley's mind never wandered. During the Sixers' thirteen playoff games, he grew from being a good rookie to a great one. He had the most rebounds on his team in ten of those thirteen games. He averaged 15 points a game.

In one opening-round win against the Milwaukee Bucks, Barkley scored 19 points, had 7 rebounds, and 5 blocked shots. He led a second-quarter 76ers' comeback by sinking two three-point shots. He helped stop the Bucks down the stretch with two steals. And when Bucks' forward Paul Mokeski tried to surprise the 76ers by driving right down the lane toward the basket, Barkley whacked him on the head and sent him rolling. It earned Barkley a foul, but it also scared Mokeski so much that he never again wandered close to the Philadelphia basket. "Charles saved our bacon tonight," Sixers' general manager Pat Williams said afterward. "I can't remember the last time a rookie did this well in the playoffs."

After beating the Bucks and the Washington Bullets, the 76ers lost to the Boston Celtics in the Eastern Conference Finals. For Barkley, it had been a great rookie season. When it ended, he went back to Alabama to spend the off-season relaxing. First though, Julius Erving—the teacher—had one last lesson for his star student. He warned Barkley to stay in shape during the off-season. If Barkley gained back all the weight he had worked so hard to lose, Erving said he would quickly find himself out of the NBA.

Barkley kept Dr. J's advice in mind. He worked out all summer and cut his dinner portions back from three entire pizzas to just one. He lost about ten pounds of fat. At the same time, he gained muscle and energy. The Round Mound of Rebound was no more.

Because of Barkley's great performance in the playoffs the year before, the Sixers gave him a much larger role at the start of the 1985–86 season. Erving was moved from forward to guard, giving Barkley more room to work under the other team's basket. And Moses Malone was moved outside a few feet, giving Barkley a chance to grab more rebounds.

The plan worked. Barkley averaged 20 points per game in 1985–86. He finished second in the NBA in rebounding, behind only Laimbeer. By the end of the season, the team that had belonged to Dr. J on the court now belonged to Barkley. It was as if the student had become the teacher.

"We have seen the future and he wears No. 34," Williams told a national TV audience at the end of the season. "Charles might be the best athlete in America. Can you think of anyone else with that size, that speed, that agility? Charles is in charge."

Barkley had to be even more in charge the next season. Sixers' coaches decided that Malone, a slow player, kept Barkley from running his fastest on the court. So before the 1986–87 season, they traded Malone to the Washington Bullets. The trade was not a good one, however. The player that Philadelphia got in return, center Jeff Ruland, injured his knee, and played just five games for the 76ers.

Andrew Toney, the 76ers' sharp-shooting guard, also got injured and stopped playing. Veteran forward Bobby Jones retired. Most importantly, Erving was thirty-six years old and losing speed. Early in the season, he announced it would be his last.

Barkley was frustrated. When he joined the pros, his teammates included some of the greatest players in NBA history. Now most of those men were gone. The young players who replaced them were not nearly as talented.

The changes showed on the court. The Sixers fell from 58 wins in Barkley's rookie year to 54 wins in 1985–86, and then to 45 wins in 1986–87. The next year, they won just 36 of the 83 regular-season games.

Certainly, no one could blame Barkley for the 76ers' tumble. Even as the team got worse, he kept getting better. His scoring rose in each of his first four seasons. In his third year, he became the shortest player ever to lead the NBA in rebounds. For three straight years, he won the NBA's Pivotal Player Award for all-around greatness. He earned a new nickname—"Sir Charles." "He honks his horn and everybody gets out of the way," said Bob Bass, general manager of the San Antonio Spurs. "If somebody tries to take a charge with Barkley, I believe it's going to be their last game."

One of the most memorable moments from Barkley's early career was the 1986 playoffs against the Bucks. Moses Malone was injured just before the playoffs, leaving Barkley to face the Bucks front line by himself. Milwaukee used three seven-footers—Paul Mokeski, Randy Breuer, and Alton Lister—but they could not control Barkley. He averaged 15 rebounds and 28 points over the seven-game series. He also played a remarkable 45 minutes per game. The pace finally caught up with him in Game 7, when he tired and the Sixers lost a 113–112 heartbreaker. Barkley worried afterward that he had let his teammates down. All of them knew, however, that without Barkley, they would not even have reached Game 7.

Two things make Barkley a special basketball player. The

Determined to get inside, Charles Barkley drives his opponent backwards toward the basket.

first is his desire. Barkley says he plays hard because he wants to be special. He doesn't want people to say, "Charles is a good player." He wants them to say, "Charles is the best."

Anyone needing proof of his pride only has to look at Barkley up close. Ugly scratches crisscross his upper arms and shoulders. They are the result of thousands of battles under the backboard in which players claw for rebounds. Barkley knows that he could move away and get fewer scratches. But he also would get fewer rebounds.

The second special thing about Barkley is his style. Most basketball players are tall and trim and graceful looking. Barkley is none of those things. Sometimes he plays like a rhino, charging straight ahead with its wide body, butting anyone who dares to get in the way. Other times he is as quick as a mousetrap, surprising sleeker opponents by beating them to the ball. He can dribble behind his back just like a guard. And he can dunk with such force that he can bend the 2,200-pound iron basket supports.

Dunking is what he enjoys most. Remember the little boy who had trouble leaping over his backyard fence? Today, he is one of the most feared dunkers in the NBA. "I'm like winter," Barkley once said. "You know I'm coming, but there's nothing you can do to stop me."

# Chapter 4

Most NBA players go their whole career without winning a league championship. All-time greats George Gervin, Alex English, and Adrian Dantley—each played more than a dozen years—yet were never part of a title team. Current stars Patrick Ewing, Karl Malone, and Shaquille O'Neal have never gotten their championship ring. Charles Barkley also falls into this group. And he does not like it.

"Hey, all I want to do is win," he once told reporters. "Anybody who doesn't like it can just get out of the way. I want to win an NBA title. Not a day goes by that I don't think about it. I'm gonna do it, too. Either that or die trying."

Whether Barkley makes it remains to be seen. The NBA has twenty-nine teams, and only one gets to carry home the trophy each year. In the last thirteen seasons, just five teams—the Boston Celtics, Los Angeles Lakers, Detroit Pistons, Chicago Bulls, and Houston Rockets—have had a turn.

The longer Barkley stayed with the Philadelphia 76ers, the worse his chances seemed to get. After Julius Erving retired in 1987, Barkley was named captain of the team. Yet it was a team in slow decline. Some of the Sixers' older veterans, such as point guard Mo Cheeks and power forward Rick Mahorn, were slowing down. And the younger players brought in to improve the club, such as guard Johnny Dawkins and forward Ron Anderson, proved to be average at best. The team's first-round draft picks turned out to be disasters.

The Sixers finished with a winning record in 1988–89 and actually won the Atlantic Division the next season. However, they got knocked out of the playoffs early both times. They were no longer regarded as being the NBA's elite clubs.

How could Barkley help? He was already giving 100 percent on the court, and truly, had emerged as one of the three or four best players in the NBA. What more could he do?

Barkley came up with an idea. He offered to take a pay cut to give the team more money to spend on other new players. He would give back $250,000 of his $2 million salary if the Sixers would use it to add another good player.

The club was pleased with Barkley's offer, but decided not to take him up on it. Barkley was worth the money he was getting, said Coach Jimmy Lynam. To pay him less would be unfair. So things just got more frustrating. The Sixers' record dropped nine games in 1990–91, and another nine the following season. In 1992, they missed the NBA playoffs, which Barkley called, "the most embarrassing moment of my life."

That summer, Barkley helped win a championship—but not for Philadelphia. He was one of twelve NBA stars named to represent the United States Olympic team in men's basketball. The squad was dubbed the Dream Team, and it was a good nickname. These dozen players combined so much talent that it seemed such a group could exist only in someone's dreams.

Charles Barkley is pictured with legendary hoops player Wilt
Chamberlain. In the 1991 NBA All-Star Game, Barkley grabbed 22
rebounds to tie Chamberlain's record.

There was Michael Jordan, the acrobatic superstar from the Chicago Bulls. And Larry Bird, who was perhaps the best clutch shooter in the sport's history. At center, there were two seven-foot all-stars—Patrick Ewing of the New York Knicks and David Robinson of the San Antonio Spurs.

And there was Barkley, the thundering dunker, the bubbly loudmouth, the heart and soul of the Olympic team. He was the team's top scorer. Sometimes, as always, Barkley went too far—such as when he elbowed the chest of an opponent from Angola. Yet everything he did was for the purpose of helping his team. "I've never met a player who wants to win so badly," said Magic Johnson, the great point guard who was on the Dream Team. "To be honest, he scares the rest of us. I'm afraid to let him down."

The Dream Team proudly brought home the Olympic Gold Medal. They won every game easily. Barkley, who had been cut from the 1984 Olympic team by Coach Bob Knight, said that representing his country was the greatest moment of his life. Now he had just one goal left—to win an NBA Championship.

He was nearing the age of thirty and knew that he only had a few good years of basketball left in his battered body. And he came to realize that the Sixers were getting further and further away from any chance of competing for the title. So Barkley asked to be traded. "I'm not playing for the money or the fun of it," he said. "I'm only playing to win. Unfortunately, that has to be somewhere else than Philadelphia."

Before the 1992–93 season, Sixers owner Harold Katz fulfilled Barkley's request. He traded Barkley to the Phoenix Suns in return for three players—guard Jeff Hornacek, forward Tim Perry, and center Andrew Lang.

Barkley was thrilled. He had gone from a losing club to one of pro basketball's best. He was in a new city with a new team starting a new life. The Suns had won 17 more games than the 76ers the previous year and went to the NBA playoff semifinals. The club included Kevin Johnson, a smart, lightning-quick point guard and small forward Dan Majerle, one of basketball's top long-range shooters. The team also included Danny Ainge and Tom Chambers, solid veterans who knew how to win.

Before the season started, Suns general manager Cotton Fitzsimmons took Barkley on a tour of the team's brand-new America West Arena. Fitzsimmons pointed to the 20,000 seats and said they had all been sold before the trade, so Barkley had nothing to do with it. Fitzsimmons said all the bricks had been laid, all the mortar spread. Barkley had nothing to do with that either. Other Suns teams had built the building with their success. Barkley had had no part. "There is one thing, though," Fitzsimmons said. "Look at the ceiling. See what's missing."

A championship flag. Barkley could do something about that. The thought sent a pleasant jolt through his body.

The fans who packed the arena immediately adored their new star in the No. 34 jersey. Barkley loved them right back. "It's sunny every day here," Barkley said. "I'm not just talking about the weather, either. I'm talking about the people, too."

His happiness showed on the basketball court. Barkley's game was reborn. He was scoring close to 26 points per game and grabbing more than 12 rebounds. Sure, the old injuries still nagged—a swollen elbow here or twisted thumb there. He had to follow every game with a 20-minute stay in the Jacuzzi, soaking out the pains along with his yellow rubber duck. Yet, overall, he felt ten years younger. And, once again, playing basketball was fun.

"Charles is the funnest guy I've ever played with," said Ainge. "He knows how to joke and have a good time. When

The Philadelphia 76ers traded Barkley to the Phoenix Suns in 1992 to give him a chance to compete for the NBA title.

the game begins, he's all business. What more could anyone ask for?" Nothing more. The Suns were rebuilt around Barkley in 1992–93. He was the foundation of the offense. The other players—some of them stars in their own right—knew that their new job was to get the ball to Barkley whenever possible. The already-good team got so much better that it boasted the NBA's best record that season. In the end, the Suns won 62 games and lost just 20.

Heading into the playoffs, the Suns were regarded as one of just a handful of teams with a chance to win the league championship. The Chicago Bulls, led by Jordan and forward Scottie Pippen, had won the title the two previous seasons. The New York Knicks, with center Patrick Ewing, was the only other team to win 60 regular-season games. The Houston Rockets, with all-star center Hakeem Olajuwon, had a shot as well. Barkley was psyched. As a young player in Philadelphia, his team had come so close. Now his chance had come again.

It was not a smooth ride. In the first round of the playoffs, the Suns somehow lost the first two games to the lowly Los Angeles Lakers. They were a game from being eliminated! Then Barkley took control. In the third game, with the score tied 60–60, Barkley went up for a rebound surrounded by three taller Lakers players. Somehow, he grabbed the ball. Spinning around in midair, he knocked all three Lakers to the ground. He returned to the air for a thundering slam dunk. The Suns never looked back, winning that game and the next two to take the series.

In the next round, the Suns disposed of David Robinson's San Antonio Spurs, four games to two. The series ended with a 102–100 game that Barkley won with a 20-foot jump shot with just three seconds left. The ball rattled around the rim and bounced three feet in the air before coming back down through the hoop. "I had it all the way," joked Barkley.

After the final game of that series, NBA Commissioner David Stern called Barkley with a bit of news. He had been named the league's Most Valuable Player for the 1992–93 season.

"Congratulations," Stern said. "How do you feel?"

"Tired," Barkley said. "But not too tired to keep playing."

He and his teammates then went out and beat the Seattle SuperSonics, four games to three. The Sonics tried double-teaming and sometimes triple-teaming Barkley to slow him down. That's okay, Barkley said. He simply passed the ball to unguarded teammates who took easy, open shots.

That left only the Chicago Bulls between Barkley and his much-coveted title. The Suns lost the first two games at home. Then they won a thrilling, triple-overtime game at the Chicago Stadium. Playing with an aching elbow that he had injured diving for a ball, Barkley battled Chicago center Bill Cartwright for rebounds. He tried defending Michael Jordan—an impossible job, for sure, but one he was willing to attempt. He drove so hard to the basket in that game that he sent defender Scottie Pippen flying into the first row of seats.

The Bulls won Game 4, putting Barkley and the Suns on the verge of elimination. Yet Phoenix fought back. Barkley refused to be denied on the night of Game 5, which was played back in Chicago. He scored 45 points and grabbed 14 rebounds. He dunked the ball, tossed in rebounds, and even hit a rare three-pointer. The Suns won the game to stay alive.

In the end, Chicago was just too tough. The Bulls had not won the two previous titles by being lucky. They rallied in Game 6, winning 99–98. It was a heartbreaker for Barkley. In many ways, 1992–93 was his greatest season. He was honored

Charles Barkley was selected as the Most Valuable Player for the 1992–93 NBA season.

as the league's top player. His scoring and rebounding were up from previous years. And he had come so close to winning the title he dreamed of for so long. "It hurts to go home without the championship trophy," he said. "But I know now that this club is good enough to do it. What do you think, next year?"

# *Chapter 5*

In some ways, Charles Barkley is like most athletes. First, he has beaten great odds to become a professional. Second, he plays his sport to win. Third, his chief goal is to get a championship for his team.

That's all on the court. Off the court, Charles Barkley is different. Other athletes speak cautiously. They answer reporters' questions by giving safe responses. They talk about "Winning one game at a time" or "giving 110 percent." Those answers don't really mean anything or stir up trouble.

Charles Barkley is not like that. His answers are never predictable or boring. Instead, they are the truth as he sees it. Barkley says whatever is on his mind. Usually, he does not think about what the results might be.

In some ways, this trait makes Charles Barkley a refreshing superstar. Who else would say, "If I was seven feet tall, I would be illegal in three states?" Who else could call Larry Bird, "the most obnoxious man I ever played against" and get away with it? Certainly, Charles Barkley is an honest man. His words may be controversial, but they come straight from his heart.

A few times, though, Barkley's words and deeds have gotten him into trouble. He has been known to criticize his teammates and swear at fans. He often argues with referees. The NBA commissioner keeps a behavior file on each player in the league. One suspects that Barkley's file takes up a whole drawer. He has been suspended for fighting with opponents, for arguing with fans, and once, for spitting into the crowd. He has said he was sorry each time. He also said he has no plans to change his personality.

Barkley likes to tell people that he is a basketball player— not a politician. In other words, he doesn't have to please the public to win. He just has to do his job. The day that fans in other cities start tossing him flowers, Barkley says, is the day he'll know it's time to retire.

The funny thing about it is that, away from the arena, Charles Barkley is one of the nicest men in sports. Just ask new teammates who end up staying at his house—nicknamed "Hotel Barkley"—until they can find a place to live. Or ask the sick children whom he visits in hospitals. Or ask anyone who has seen this giant of a man cuddle his young daughter.

"Many players are really jerks who want people to think they're nice," said Dave Kosky, a former NBA public relations director. "But Charles is a nice guy who wants people to think he's a jerk. It's as if he doesn't want to lose that 'bad-guy' image."

In arenas on the road, Barkley is cast as the villain. He is probably booed more loudly than almost any other player in the NBA. He takes the heat, actually seeming to enjoy it. On his home court, of course, he is a fan favorite.

Frequently, Barkley will play to the balcony like an actor in a play. He raises a clenched fist after a dunk or pats the

Charles Barkley has a very competitive spirit. Occasionally, Barkley's emotions have led him to do things that have gotten him into trouble.

referee on the rear when he believes the official has made a good call—even if it's against him. During some road games, he'll carry on a running argument with heckling fans from the opening tip-off until the final buzzer. He'll grin at the crowd or stick out his tongue.

That's all in good fun. However, a few times it has gone beyond that. Once, in early 1991, Barkley lost control of his emotions during a game against the New Jersey Nets at the Meadowlands Arena. A fan sitting courtside kept shouting racial insults at Barkley. Finally, in the fourth quarter, Barkley had heard enough. With play stopped for a foul shot, Barkley walked past the screaming man and spit toward him. He missed his target and hit an eight-year-old girl who was there with her family. Immediately, it seemed, the entire crowd of 15,000 began booing Barkley.

Barkley felt terrible. Not only had he done something wrong by trying to spit at the fan, but he had hit a little girl. Afterward, he said he had snapped and admitted it was a stupid thing to do. He called up the girl the next day to apologize. She forgave him. However, the NBA was not so forgiving. It fined Barkley $45,000 and suspended him for one game, which his team lost.

When Barkley loses control, it all stems from his tremendous desire to win. He is a passionate player who cannot stand losing and must get the most out of every minute. When he makes a mistake, he grabs his head in despair. When he power dunks over Patrick Ewing, he pumps his fist and jumps for joy.

Barkley said he does these things not to show off, but to get himself pumped up. Besides, he asks, what's wrong with showing his excitement when he makes a good play? And why should he care if the other teams' fans like him?

More important to Barkley is what his opponents think of

him. The answer: They may not like him, but they respect him. Five times, they have voted him to the All-NBA team. Most say they do not enjoy playing against him because he is so rough.

"He's really hyper, real intense," said Dominique Wilkins formerly of the Atlanta Hawks. "Sometimes, his temper really gets him going. You know, he gets a look in his eyes and you know he is ready to play."

Larry Bird once said he understands that Barkley's bluster is part of his game. "I'm the type of person who doesn't always say the right things myself," Bird said. "But I never apologize for what I've said, even though I may regret them. The best thing you can do is be your own person. And Charles is definitely his own person."

Bird has seen Barkley's antics close up. A few years ago, Bird was on the foul line in the final seconds of a tight Celtics-76ers game at the Philadelphia Spectrum. Even though he was the NBA's best foul shooter at the time, Bird missed the first of two free throws. Barkley, standing nearby, leaned forward and grabbed his throat, giving Bird the "choke" sign. Bird was so rattled that he missed the second shot—allowing the Sixers to win the game.

The truth is, Charles Barkley completely changes when the game is over. There is a fire that burns inside him that makes him want to win. Yet there is also a big heart. Barkley adores those fans who adore him. He spends hours signing autographs or talking about basketball with perfect strangers who approach him in airports or shopping malls.

He also loves to help kids. One time, the Phoenix Suns got a call from a high school basketball coach in Florida. The coach said he had cut a boy from the team. Now the boy was talking about dropping out of school. Charles Barkley is the

As part of his campaign against drugs, Barkley got to meet First Lady Nancy Reagan in 1987.

boy's hero, the coach said. Would Barkley mind talking to the boy for just a few minutes?

The Suns arranged to have Barkley call from their office. However, the boy wasn't there. So that night, Barkley went home and spent an hour on the phone with the boy. He straightened him out and got him back into the classroom.

"As a person, he's a tremendous human being," said Chuck Person, his old college teammate and fellow NBA player. "He's kind of shy, I guess, laid-back. He's a fun-loving guy. He's dedicated to his family." During games, Person said, Barkley plays like an angry bear. Yet off the floor, Person calls him a teddy bear.

Certainly, he's that way with his family. Barkley's favorite times are when he's alone with his wife Maureen and his young daughter Christiana. Celebrity life can be exciting, but it can also be tiring. Imagine having people come up to you all day asking for your autograph or wanting to shake your hand. Sometimes it may be fun. Other times you might want to be left alone with your family.

Barkley and his wife were married in 1989. Any marriage can be stressful, but Barkley's was even more so. He is black and his wife is white. Every so often when they go out in public together, they hear whispers or see angry stares.

At first, that made Barkley angry. Now, he says, he just ignores the people who disapprove.

"For someone to dislike another person because of skin color is silly," he said. "What we're talking about here is pretty simple: It's two people who love each other. Our family and friends understand. I can't worry about pleasing other people." That sums up the straightforward Barkley approach: You can't please everyone, so you have to do what seems right to you.

When people tell him that his interracial marriage can't

Charles Barkley's latest challenge is to help lead the Houston Rockets to an NBA championship.

work, Barkley sees that as a challenge. And remember, Charles Barkley's life has been a series of challenges. He has learned to meet them—and to beat them. It's similar to the time when people told him he was too short or too fat to make it as a player. He proved them wrong then. He met that challenge. Now, he says, his biggest challenge is to finally win an NBA championship.

# *Chapter 6*

Charles Barkley did not know it at the end of the 1992–93 season, but the Suns would not return to the NBA Finals during his next three seasons in Phoenix. The Suns remained one of the league's top teams. But each year, it seemed, they would hit a wall in the playoffs, bowing out against a tougher, more talented club.

Sure, Barkley was disappointed. But he was learning to look at his career in perspective. For ten straight seasons, he was selected to play in the NBA All-Star Game. That was something to be proud of. A 1994 article in *Sport* magazine rated him as the best-ever power forward in basketball—better than Karl Malone, better than Kevin McHale, better than Elvin Hayes. In 1996, he scored his 20,000th point. Only two dozen players had ever reached that mark in the history of the league. Being a great player over a short period is one thing; being a great player over a long career is something else.

Not that it was ever easy. Barkley spent his games banging bodies under the backboards. He continued to dive on the floor after loose balls. That style of play earned him frequent

Struggling to get to the basket, Charles Barkley fights for an open shot against Bo Outlaw of the Los Angeles Clippers. In 1994, Barkley was named the best power forward of all time by *Sport* magazine.

injuries. One year, his elbow ached for months. Another year, Harvey Grant of the Portland Trailblazers accidentally elbowed Barkley over the eye, causing two weeks of double vision. And Barkley's back always ached.

Charles Barkley kept playing hard—it was the only way he knew how to play. But the injuries mounted up. Late in the 1993–94 season, when his back hurt so badly that he couldn't play in the playoffs, he announced plans to play one more year and then retire. Of course, when the time came a year later, he changed his mind. "For years, I thought that I had a hold on basketball," he said. "It turns out, basketball has a hold on me." Three more times in the next three years, he said he would soon quit the game. Three more times, he ended up deciding to stick around.

Barkley's great talent and his outrageous personality always made him a favorite of advertisers looking for an athlete to sell their products. He has done commercials for everything from sneakers to deodorant to hamburgers. Adults have always laughed at his sense of humor. Children have always looked up to him.

But in 1993, Barkley caused a stir. He said that he did not think kids should try to be like him. "I am not a role model," he said. "It is not my job to raise anybody's kids. That is the parents' job. My job is to wreak havoc on the basketball court."

Barkley explained that too many children thought they could be like him and make it in the NBA. Only one out of one million young players ever makes it to the pros, he said. So parents should steer their children in other directions. Push them to be doctors and lawyers and teachers, he said. Don't let them quit school for basketball.

In that regard, Barkley seemed to be making sense. But many fans—and some fellow players—did not like what he had to say. Karl Malone of the Utah Jazz said that Barkley could not accept the fame and high pay of his job without also accepting the responsibilities that came along with it. "We do not choose to be role models," Malone said. "We are chosen. Our only choice is whether to be a good role model or a bad one."

Funny thing is, Barkley is usually a great role model. He enjoys people, especially young people. Each year, he hosts a celebrity golf tournament to raise money to fight childhood illnesses. Barkley invites hundreds of kids onto the golf course to meet their favorite athletes. Any player who is not friendly to the kids does not get invited back the following year.

Many big-time athletes learn to hide from normal life. They ride in limousines, hire bodyguards to keep people away, and stay locked in hotel rooms ordering room service. Not Barkley. He says he would go crazy if he did not get to lead a normal life—or at least as normal as possible. So he eats in public restaurants, dances in clubs, and mingles with his fans. He would rather go to a movie theater than rent a movie to watch at home. He almost never refuses anyone asking for an autograph.

Barkley always felt comfortable in Phoenix. He liked the city and its people. And, during his four years there, the Suns averaged 55 wins and just 27 losses a season. But, by the end of the 1995–96 season, the team—and Barkley—had to make a tough decision. The Suns were getting older and less talented. Barkley could stay and be part of a rebuilding program (like the one he had gone through in Philadelphia), or move on to another new club. If the Suns traded Barkley, they could land several top prospects who might help them in the future.

Barkley and the Suns front office argued over the team's

At the end of the 1996 season, the Suns were an aging team. Suns'
management decided to trade Barkley to the Houston Rockets for
younger players.

direction. He wanted to stay, but only if owner Jerry Colangelo promised to sign top free agents and give Barkley a new, long-term contract. Colangelo decided he would rather go with youth. So, on August 19, 1996, Barkley was traded for the second time in his career. He was sent to the Houston Rockets in exchange for four players—guard Sam Cassell, and forwards Robert Horry, Chucky Brown, and Mark Bryant.

The Rockets were already a great team. They had won two NBA titles without Barkley. Their lineup had two future Hall of Famers—center Hakeem Olajuwon and guard Clyde Drexler. What could he add? Barkley knew he had to change his game. Instead of scoring, he focused on rebounding. "I figured I have two choices," he said. "I could stand here and pick my nose. Or I could do what the team needs."

The plan worked. The Rockets won 21 of their first 23 games in 1996. Barkley was jumping like a kangaroo. Then, once again, the injuries came. Barkley missed 29 games with a sore hip and a bad knee. Houston lost 13 of those games.

He came back just in time for the playoffs. The Rockets swept past the Minnesota Timberwolves and then eked out a seventh-game victory over Shawn Kemp and the Seattle SuperSonics. Long after one of those wins, when his teammates were headed home, Barkley was still running wind sprints across the court. Did he think that, at age thirty-four, he was going to get himself in much better condition? Probably not. More likely, it was a message to teammates not to ever slack off.

The Rockets' season ended when they ran up against the tough Utah Jazz, led by 1997 NBA Most Valuable Player Karl Malone. It was a tough six-game series, marred by a scuffle between Barkley and Utah guard John Stockton. Years earlier, the two men had been friends and teammates on the U.S. Olympic team. "He's not my buddy when he's wearing a different colored uniform," Barkley told reporters after the fight. Later, the two men apologized to each other and shook hands.

After five games, the Rockets trailed, 3–2. One more loss and their season would end. Game 6, at the Summit in Houston, was a classic. Barkley put in 20 points for the Rockets, who led for most of the game. But the Jazz climbed back. With less than three seconds remaining, the score was tied, 100–100. Karl Malone set a pick, and Stockton drove toward the hoop and then pulled up near the three-point line. Stockton got off a clean shot before Barkley could get over to cover him. It swished through the basket at the buzzer.

Once again, Barkley was kept from his goal of a championship. After the game, he took the blame for the loss, saying he should have run through Malone if necessary. Of course, reporters asked if he planned to retire.

This time, he promised to keep playing. Barkley said that he no longer regarded himself among the top three or four players in the NBA. But he still put himself in the top ten. "As long as I'm playing well," he said, "I'm going to play."

The 1997–98 season proved to be a rough year for Barkley and the Rockets. The team was hurt by injuries and finished a mediocre, 41–41. Barkley himself missed fourteen games, but finished the year averaging 15.2 points, and a tremendous 11.7 rebounds per game. The Rockets reached the playoffs but were eliminated in the first round, by the Utah Jazz for the second straight year.

Maybe he will be near the top of his game for a few more seasons. And after that? Barkley insists he is not kidding people when he says he may return to his home in Alabama and run for governor.

"I feel like the blacks and poor people there don't have the pride and self-esteem they need to push themselves," he said.

In 1997, Charles Barkley helped the Houston Rockets reach the Western Conference Finals, where they fell to the Utah Jazz in six games.

"I don't think they really realize how big a chance they have in life. So, if I win, I would get on television every day and just try to uplift them. I would tell them they can be successful. They can be what they want to be."

"I don't think they understand that the President of the United States was a poor kid from a small town. Charles Barkley was a poor kid from a small town. Michael Jordan is from a little town. People don't realize what chance they have in life because they've been beat down so long. If I could get on television and tell them, 'Hey, you're just as good as everybody out there. You've just got to push yourself and you have a chance.' Well, that would mean I'm a good person doing my job."

Few people do their job as well as Charles Barkley. And there is no doubt that he has always been a good person.

# College

| Year | Team | GP | FG% | REB | PTS | AVG |
|------|------|-----|------|------|------|------|
| 1981–82 | Auburn | 28 | .595 | 275 | 356 | 12.7 |
| 1982–83 | Auburn | 28 | .644 | 266 | 404 | 14.4 |
| 1983–84 | Auburn | 28 | .638 | 265 | 423 | 15.1 |
| *Totals* | | 84 | .636 | 806 | 1,183 | 14.1 |

# NBA

| Year | Team | GP | FG% | REB | AST | STL | BLK | PTS | AVG |
|------|------|-----|------|------|------|------|------|------|------|
| 1984–85 | Philadelphia | 82 | .545 | 703 | 155 | 95 | 80 | 1,148 | 14.0 |
| 1985–86 | Philadelphia | 80 | .572 | 1,026 | 312 | 173 | 125 | 1,603 | 20.0 |
| 1986–87 | Philadelphia | 68 | .594 | 994 | 331 | 119 | 104 | 1,564 | 23.0 |
| 1987–88 | Philadelphia | 80 | .587 | 951 | 254 | 100 | 103 | 2,264 | 28.3 |
| 1988–89 | Philadelphia | 79 | .579 | 986 | 325 | 126 | 67 | 2,037 | 25.8 |
| 1989–90 | Philadelphia | 79 | .600 | 909 | 307 | 148 | 50 | 1,989 | 25.2 |
| 1990–91 | Philadelphia | 67 | .570 | 680 | 284 | 110 | 33 | 1,849 | 27.6 |
| 1991–92 | Philadelphia | 75 | .552 | 830 | 308 | 136 | 44 | 1,730 | 23.1 |
| 1992–93 | Phoenix | 76 | .520 | 928 | 385 | 119 | 74 | 1,944 | 25.6 |
| 1993–94 | Phoenix | 65 | .495 | 727 | 296 | 101 | 37 | 1,402 | 21.6 |
| 1994–95 | Phoenix | 68 | .486 | 756 | 276 | 110 | 45 | 1,561 | 23.0 |
| 1995–96 | Phoenix | 71 | .500 | 821 | 262 | 114 | 56 | 1,649 | 23.2 |
| 1996–97 | Houston | 53 | .484 | 716 | 248 | 69 | 25 | 1,016 | 19.2 |
| 1997–98 | Houston | 68 | .485 | 794 | 217 | 71 | 28 | 1,036 | 15.2 |
| *Totals* | | 1,011 | .544 | 11,812 | 3,960 | 1,591 | 871 | 22,792 | 22.5 |

GP=Games Played      AST=Assists      PTS=Points
FG%=Field Goal Percentage      STL=Steals      AVG=Points Per Game
REB=Rebounds      BLK=Blocks

# *Where to Write Charles Barkley:*

Mr. Charles Barkley
c/o Houston Rockets
The Summit
10 Greenway Plaza
Houston, TX  77046

*On the Internet at:*

http://www.nba.com/playerfile/charles_barkley.htm
http://www.nba.com/Rockets

# *Index*

## A

Ainge, Danny, 9, 37
Alabama, 28, 58
America West Arena, 37
Anderson, Ron, 34
Angola, 36
Atlanta Hawks, 47
Auburn University, 13, 18–21

## B

Barkley, Christiana, 49
Barkley, Maureen, 49
Bass, Bob, 30
Bird, Larry, 36, 43, 47
Boston Celtics, 24, 28, 33, 47
Breuer, Randy, 30
Brown, Chucky, 57
Bryant, Mark, 57

## C

Cartwright, Bill, 40
Cassell, Sam, 57
Chambers, Tom, 13, 37
Cheeks, Maurice, 24, 34
Chicago Bulls, 7, 11, 23, 33, 36, 39, 40
Chicago Stadium, 9, 11
Colangelo, Jerry, 57
Coupland, Bill, 15
Cunningham, Billy, 27, 28

## D

Dantley, Adrian, 33
Dawkins, Johnny, 34
Detroit Pistons, 28, 33
"Dream Team," 34, 36
Drexler, Clyde, 57

## E

Edwards, Adolphus, 16
Edwards, Johnnie, 16
English, Alex, 33
Ensley (Ala.) High School, 18
Erving, Julius, 24, 26, 28, 29, 33
Ewing, Patrick, 21, 33, 36, 39, 46

## F

Fitzsimmons, Cotton, 37

## G

Georgetown Hoyas, 21
Gervin, George, 33
Glenn, Charcey, 16, 18
Glenn, Clee, 16
Grant, Harvey, 54
Grant, Horace, 9

## H

Hardaway, Penny, 11
Hayes, Elvin, 52
Hornacek, Jeff, 36
Horry, Robert, 57
Houston Rockets, 11, 23, 33, 39, 57–58
Houston Summit, 58
Hurt, Bobby Lee, 18

## J

Johnson, Kevin, 7, 37
Johnson, Magic, 36
Jones, Bobby, 24, 26, 29
Jordan, Michael, 7, 11, 13, 23, 36, 39, 40, 58

## K

Katz, Harold, 36
Kemp, Shawn, 11, 57

Knight, Bob, 36
Kosky, Dave, 44

**L**

Laimbeer, Bill, 28, 29
Lang, Andrew, 36
Leeds, Alabama, 15–16
Leeds (Ala.) High School, 15, 16, 18
Lister, Alton, 30
Los Angeles Clippers, 24
Los Angeles Lakers, 9, 24, 33, 39

**M**

Mahorn, Rick, 34
Majerle, Dan, 7, 37
Malone, Karl, 33, 52, 55, 57, 58
Malone, Moses, 24, 29, 30
McHale, Kevin, 52
Meadowlands Arena, 46
Milwaukee Bucks, 28, 30
Minnesota Timberwolves, 57
Mokeski, Paul, 28, 30

**N**

NBA draft, 23
NBA Most Valuable Player Award, 9, 14, 40, 57
NBA Pivotal Player Award, 30
New Jersey Nets, 46
New York Knicks, 36, 39
Nigeria, 23

**O**

Olajuwon, Hakeem, 23, 39, 57
Olympics, 1992 Summer, 34, 36, 57
O'Neal, Shaquille, 33

**P**

Perkins, Sam, 23

Perry, Tim, 36
Person, Chuck, 49
Philadelphia, Pennsylvania, 26, 36, 39, 55
Philadelphia 76ers, 9, 23, 24–32, 33–34, 36, 47
Phoenix, Arizona, 55
Phoenix Suns, 7–14, 36–42, 47, 52, 55
Pippen, Scottie, 39
Portland Trailblazers, 54
Pro Basketball Hall of Fame, 14

**R**

Robertson, Alvin, 23
Robinson, David, 36, 39
Ruland, Jeff, 29

**S**

San Antonio Spurs, 9, 30, 36, 39
Seattle SuperSonics, 9, 40, 57
Smith, Sonny, 18–19, 21
Southeastern Conference, 21
Sport magazine, 52
Stern, David, 40
Stockton, John, 23, 57, 58

**T**

Tomjanovich, Rudy, 11
Toney, Andrew, 24, 29
Tuscaloosa, Alabama, 18

**U**

Utah Jazz, 55, 57–58

**W**

Washington Bullets, 28, 29
Westphal, Paul, 7
Wilkins, Dominique, 47
Williams, Pat, 28, 29